Reframing Autism

The Promise of Acceptance

Tony Rice

United States Copyright

TXu002319067-2022-5-15

TABLE OF CONTENTS

DEDICATION

I dedicate this book to my son TJ and to my daughter Courtney.

TJ, autism is a very real part of your life, and yet you have never permitted autism to define who you are. Your goals and your dreams are ambitious, and with your unrelenting drive, I know that you will exceed them all.

Courtney, both time and money have been in limited supply as we have navigated the family challenges that go along with an autism journey.

You have never made excuses. Quite the opposite. Your natural disposition has propelled you to excel and to lead throughout your academic life.

Courtney is currently president of the University of Missouri Veterinary School - Class of 2024. I am in awe.

You are my greatest loves, and the source of my greatest joy.

I also dedicate this book to each and every autistic human being who yearns for you to embrace the perspectives that are shared within these pages.

PREFACE

Nearly eight years ago I began speaking with thousands of people to include everyday acquaintances, autism individuals/families, and hundreds of experts, about issues surrounding the state of autism perceptions and messaging among our society today.

The more I talked with people, the more it became clear that we as a society are following old habits. Old habits that, when studied and reformed, will set into motion greatly enhanced levels of connection. A byproduct of these greater connections will be scores of new employment opportunities for the autism community, and for greatly expanded collaborations among our society as a whole.

I am an autism father of twenty-five plus years and I too was finally diagnosed as mildly autistic about ten years ago. I am a certified Special Needs Life Quality Coach. I have done a thirty-minute program on our PBS Channel-9 station here in St Louis on autism advocacy 17 years ago. I have been invited back to do a program when this book gets released.

I have also attended a lot of conferences and support groups over the years. In addition, have been very fortunate to discuss this specific mission with Temple Grandin, more on her later, at two recent conferences.

On my inside, I truly feel like I am one of those effervescent, Keith Urban sorts of chap, but truth be told, my resting facial expression can scare people. For many autistic individuals, but not for all, this is just an autism thing. Often times, my outside expressions will very much not reflect my inside levels of optimism, hope and joy.

I once offered up my warmest smile during an awkward traffic situation and I was promptly served a middle finger in response. I thought to myself, "Yep, that's about right!".

I was also born with a bone condition that required numerous surgeries as a child, several of them on my knees. The function of my ankles has also been impacted. As a result, I walk, and I stand sort of funny.

I have occasionally had doubts about all of this. "Am I really the one who should be doing this?". "Does anybody really care?". "Are people truly concerned about the issues that I am bringing to light?".

Over the years, there have been days when I just mentally quit. "Enough with all of this". "It's time to quit messing around and to get back to my old career". "Phew, glad I made that decision, now I can get on with my life!". "Feels good, feels good!".

And then, inevitably, on those days that I would officially end to this mission, at least in my mind, I would do some ride-share driving and I would meet somebody who I could help. I would find myself un-quitting before I even realized was what I was doing.

From the outset I did not have a strategic, calculated plan for any of this. There are just issues surrounding the autism conversation among our society that have pestered me for many years.

It has always hurt my heart to see people **talk at** my son rather than to **speak with** him. Not because I thought they were bad or mean people, it hurt my heart because these people simply believed that this is what that they should be doing.

In 1930's America, the accepted belief was that kids who had cognitive differences should be surrendered to state institutions to be warehoused, so that those families "could have good and normal lives too". More on this later.

This systemic practice wasn't inherently evil, it was just terribly wrong. Eventually, experts recognized this, and as a result, today we have, as a society, clearly shifted away from what was once considered a best practice.

Yet today, even though anomalies and imperfections are now visible through modern MRI techniques, anomalies present in **every** human brain by the way, we as a society continue to look at individuals with sub-sets of cognitive differences, sub-sets, like autism, through some form of a we/they filter.

Also, the messaging among our society paints a picture that says autism is incredibly, even impossibly complex. But there are fundamental, scientifically sound facts available about autism that can fully explain autism. Fundamental facts that virtually anybody can understand with confidence.

And when we can have fundamental, confident understandings about autism, then we/they dynamics no longer makes any sense.

If you are reading this book there is a pretty good chance that one or many beautiful autistic souls have been a part of your life. And if autistic individuals have impacted your life, there is a strong chance that your personal autism experiences and your unique autism stories are lovely expressions of what is truly good about our humanity.

These are stories that have already been written, and these stories are written with the purest kinds of love. When these special stories have been written, we are understandably reluctant to re-write any element of our stories.

I believe that moms, dads, friends, acquaintances, and experts all shared those sentiments back in the 1930's too. They were operating on the very best of motives, relying on the best information available at that time. Yet, when new and better information became widely understood, it compelled profound change towards something better.

This tendency to protect our stories has presented significant hurdles for me over these past eight years. Without going on about this, I have an appeal for you.

Please be willing to step out of your story lines with me to contemplate some fresh insights. Insights that have been developed through lived experience, through years of research, and through thousands of interviews.

The autism conversation is, generally speaking, a young conversation. While the first autism paper was published in 1943, it was not recognized as an official diagnosis and listed within the DSM-*Diagnostic and Statistical Manual of Mental Disorders*, (For the record, I hate the term, "disorder"), until 1980.

A widely viewed movie "Rain Man" was released in 1988. This movie introduced a largely unknown term, "autism", into our mainstream lexicon. The actor Dustin Hoffman played the character Raymond, a young adult autistic guy who demonstrated remarkable savant abilities.[2]

Although the movie *Rain Man* did not provide a complete picture, it was impactful in bringing the autism conversation into greater general awareness.

My son, TJ was born in 1992. Indicators of his autism diagnosis became apparent in 1994. We started early specialized programs when he was three years old.

His official diagnosis, pervasive developmental disorder (PDD) with autistic tendencies, was provided by a neurologist in 1996.

At that time, most of the neurologists would diagnose younger kids who were autistic with a PDD qualifier. It was believed, at that time, that there were thousands of unique, one-of-a-kind types of autism. More on that later.

Thankfully, this is no longer the case. Today, there are three primary autism diagnoses that are listed within the diagnostic manual. Autism-Level 1, mild impact. Autism-Level 2, moderate impact, will benefit from some lifestyle supports, and Autism-Level 3, significant impact, will

---

[2] Savant syndrome represents up to 37% of those diagnosed with autism. James E. A. Hughes et al., "Savant Syndrome has a Distinct Psychological Profile in Autism," Molecular Autism 9, no. 53 (October 2018), https://doi.org/10.1186/s13229-018-0237-1.

require extensive lifestyle supports throughout their lifetime.

In the early days, although autism was somewhat recognized in society, it was thought to be rare. You may have heard or read about it, but you just didn't expect for it to directly impact your family.

Most of the energy at that time was directed towards research and treatment of autism. There was also anticipation that a cure should and would be found soon, if only we tried hard enough.

In hindsight, it is easy to see that there was little, if any, energy being directed toward accepting and embracing that individual as a whole and complete human being. This just had to be fixed!

The motivation to "fix this" came from a place of love. There should be no mistaking that. I think it is important to note, however, that even from a place of great love, if we aren't careful, "fix this" can quickly overshadow acceptance of the individual.

I have yet to meet a person who does not want whole and complete acceptance for who they are, right here, right now, in this moment.

Research and learning have and continue to bring tremendous benefit to the Autism community. If everybody were like me, I think that we probably would have done too much accepting, and we would not have benefitted from much of the important research that has taken place.

We need research, but I assure you, that from a perspective behind the eyes of autism, that we yearn for acceptance, first and foremost, even more. Who doesn't, right?

So then, what is the current state of the autism conversation, and where can we go from here?

I have presented my case to dozens of psychologists, neurologists, therapists, specialists, teachers, fellow travelers on the autism spectrum, and to a whole lot of you normie types.

From the outside and from the perspective of any new autism parent, autism appears frighteningly complex. Hundreds of books have been written, and entire industries seemed to have popped up out of nowhere, dedicated to treating the impacts of autism. If I were to observe all of that from the outside, it would all look pretty complicated to me too.

My career has primarily involved working within the mass retail and ecommerce trade channels. My responsibilities have included product development, retail packaging development, marketing strategy, and making sales presentations to many of the largest retailers North America.

In a mass retail environment, it is understood that you only have a fraction of a second for the consumer to glance at your product, among many other products on a shelf, to recognize what the product is, to understand the benefit of that product, and to have confidence that the product will deliver the promised benefit.

This is a lot that needs to happen within a fraction of a second. Why? Because we are all busy, too busy, overwhelmed in fact, with a constant flow of information and an endless list of things to-do. You know it; I know it; there is no surprise there.

I have also had the experience of creating a packing, shipping, and printing business. During that process I started by hiring a consultant. With his guidance, we found a great location, and we created an attractive store.

People thought that my business was a franchise, but it was actually an independent business. We had matching neon signage throughout the store. We were located on a corner with full glass front and side windows. This offered good visibility into the store from the parking lot, as well as from a busy nearby intersection.

I was excited on opening day. We had been involved in every detail of the build out project for months. All that was left to do now was to smile, to shake hands, and to make that money!

But when I clicked the dead bolt open, it was mostly calm and quiet, not a lot of business activity that day.

Through that experience, I saw first-hand how things can happen right in front of us that just don't register with us. We can so easily look right past the right now.

That work experience impacted the way that I view our current state of messaging relative to autism.

The Autism Awareness and Acceptance mantras have had a positive effect over the past twenty years or so. Clearly, we have greater awareness and acceptance. But we have to ask ourselves, precisely what are we aware of, and precisely what are we to accept?

The Autism Awareness and Autism Acceptance mantras promote admirable goals, yet in practical terms, these mantras tend to elicit a lot of guilt while delivering little practical insight towards reaching those goals.

I have always been uncomfortable attending what have seemed like gripe sessions cleverly disguised as Autism Support Groups. Not all of the groups were like that, but many of them were. I don't say this to discount the challenges, sometimes the overwhelming challenges that autism families will navigate. I say this because, let's face it, griping and guilting can be easy traps to fall into.

The one thing that griping and guilting the public at large accomplishes, with absolute certainty, is that these behaviors create walls. A message that will serve to inspire connection the one that will win hearts and minds. If guilting did the trick, I would be all for it. But since that clearly doesn't work, then we should pay attention to what will.

At the outset of this project, I was apprehensive about this autism thesis, one that is built on the principle of *simplicity*. I have tried to approach every conversation from the angle, "Am I missing something here?". Along the way, I have learned, and have sometimes adjusted the sails, yet the core basis of this approach has held firm.

I hope that you will find that these pages resonate with hope and with unrelenting optimism. This is a good news message about autistic people and about autism.

In advocating for greater autism connection among our society, I believe that we should avoid comments like, "You should", "You need to", or "I wish that you would". Instead, we should pursue themes that are affirming and inspiring. Themes like, "You can", I believe that you want to", and "Here's how". Finger wagging might feel satisfying in the moment, but I don't think it has actually been helpful in moving the ball forward.

This book is not about treating, counseling, intervening, curing, or changing any person who is on the autism spectrum. There are good people who dedicate their lives to doing that sort of work, but that is not this mission. We focus on acceptance and on human connection.

When my son was diagnosed, I questioned if I really knew who he was. Suddenly it seemed like I needed an expert to *tell* me who he was. I didn't have a confident grasp on anything at that point.

I was wrong. I had it backwards. I knew full well who my son was and who he is, but with the introduction of an autism diagnosis, I suddenly had doubts about almost everything.

Today, as I read new information, attend conferences, or view informative videos about autism, I understand that medical professionals and experts can help us to better understand important elements of *nuance* about our kids.

No expert, no study, or educational video can tell us *who* our kids are. That is our job, and our kids count on us to do that job well.

When we do our part well, then we are equipped to evaluate new information that will benefit our child's autism journey. Knowing, understanding, accepting, and embracing our kids wholly and completely as our first priority will position us to identify any new information, therapies or treatments that are beneficial, and to confidently leave behind all information, therapies or treatments that are not.

I hope this book will offer life affirming clarity for any person who engages with autistic individuals, on any level, in your daily life.

I hope that the insights offered in this book will serve as a foundational resource for any employer as you hire, manage, and/or collaborate with any autistic associate.

And parents, yes, if you receive that initial autism diagnosis for your child, I hope that you will read this book right away. Equipped with lived experience and with the insights that are shared, you can step into this unplanned, new life adventure with confidence.

There is snake oil out there. Some people make fantastical claims regarding autism treatments and even cures. Some of them might be tempting. Evaluating these treatments, with perspective, shared from behind the eyes of autism, will equip you to navigate with clarity.

As fallible, generally well-intentioned human beings, we tend to follow familiar habits right up until the point that new information, insight, and understanding compel change for something better.

It is my hope that through these pages, that you will find insights that can move elements of your beautiful stories to something even better.

Chapter 1

Societies Evolve - We Always Have

As recently as the late 1930's in America, the best thinking from the brightest, most educated, even those considered most moral among American society suggested that kids with Autism, Down Syndrome, or other cognitive differences should be surrendered to the state, to be warehoused, so that those affected families would have the opportunity to have "good and normal lives" too.

Leo Kanner is a familiar, historic figure in the autism community. As Chief of Child Psychiatry at the Johns Hopkins Hospital in Baltimore, Kanner is credited with writing the first paper on Autism, "Autistic Disturbances of Affective Contact". This was originally published in 1943.[3]

Kanner had established the very first child psychology clinic at Johns Hopkins Hospital in 1930.[4] He was also recognized as a trailblazing activist on behalf of children with cognitive differences.

---

[3] Wikipedia, s.v. "Leo Kanner," last modified February 21, 2022, https://en.wikipedia.org/wiki/Leo_Kanner#.
[4] Wikipedia, s.v. "Leo Kanner."

In 1938, Kanner confronted the accepted "best" practice of systemic institutionalization for children with cognitive differences. He audited a large state of Maryland program, exposing widespread abuse in the process. As a result, what had been accepted as a norm among polite society up until 1938, is of course, today, an unthinkable practice.

Paradigm shifts for better do happen. If this has happened before, then surely it can and will happen again.

Today, we understand a lot more about human anatomy and about human brain function. Through recently developed, new and improved fMRI techniques, we can not only view the unique anomalies that are present in the autistic brain, but we are also able to identify unique anomalies present within every human brain. No two brains are exactly alike.

Of course, we should never minimize the unique sensory intensity differences, the white matter overdevelopment, that is unique to the autistic brain. It is, however, extremely helpful to know that autism is physically present within the human brain. Autism is not optional, it cannot be wished away, it cannot be "put on hold" for a more convenient time.

When society is given permission to fully embrace this basic information, then the concept of "accommodating sensory issues" can be replaced with the concept of doing what is purely logical.

I can't tell you how many experts that I have spoken with about this specific issue over the past seven years. I keep asking the same questions, and to my amazement, I keep getting the same response.

Me - "Mr. or Ms. expert, am I missing something here?"

Expert – "Nope."

Me – "Well then this is a big deal, right? I mean, with this basic information understood, any person can have a fundamental understanding of any autistic person that they will encounter, at any level of autism impact, right?"

Expert – "Yep!"

Me – "Wow! I can't wait to tell more people!"

So then, where to begin? How about, let's begin with a highly reputable, widely accepted, unfortunate definition for autism. This one is currently published in the Merriam-Webster dictionary.

The definition will be shown in *bold italics*. I will offer some commentary as we go through each section.

": a variable <u>developmental disorder</u> that appears by age three and is characterized especially by difficulties in forming and maintaining social relationships, by impairment of the ability to communicate verbally or nonverbally, and by repetitive behavior patterns and restricted interests and activities... the chief diagnostic signs of autism are social isolation, lack of eye contact, poor language capacity and absence of empathy ..."[5]

I don't believe that Merriam-Webster publishes this definition with any sort of bad motive. It probably reflects a general understanding of autism at the time this version of the definition was published.

That said, I am surprised that this definition has not been updated and/or corrected.

---

[5] Merriam-Webster Online, s.v. "Autism," accessed February 21, 2022, https://www.merriam-webster.com/dictionary/autism.

OK, let's break it down:

: *a variable <u>developmental disorder</u>*

If every human brain contains anomalies and imperfections, then why is it that we reserve derogatory descriptors like *disorder*, only for select sub-groups like autistic people? I believe that at this point in our modern understandings about anatomy, that we can and should update these historically accepted, derogatory terms.

Difference? Sure, the term is both accurate and without a demeaning inference.

characterized especially by difficulties in forming and maintaining social relationships,

Why the disparaging perspective? It is both correct and affirming to say, "Selective in forming and maintaining social relationships."

impairment of the ability to communicate verbally or nonverbally

"Are generally more precise in verbal communication. Those with greater sensory intensity impacts may choose to communicate with more subtle, non-verbal methods."

repetitive behavior patterns and restricted interests and activities...

"Can be highly focused on specific behavior patterns, interests, or activities. This gift of focus has been responsible for many innovations, advancements, and discoveries. Inventions that have delivered great benefit modern to society."

social isolation

"Often prefer greater than average alone time in order to decompress from the enhanced sensory intensity experiences that are common with autism."

lack of eye contact

For the autistic person, what is considered to be normal eye contact can be uncomfortable due to enhanced sensory intensities. Logically, as a result, autistic individuals will often prefer less eye contact.

poor language capacity

"Precise use of language"

There are many words in the English language that are imprecise. Often times autistic people will choose better words. These words might sound complex or uncommon, but they are usually more precise and accurate.

An absence of empathy ... (Absence?!)

What?!

An absence of empathy reflects a core trait of a **sociopath**! So, there's that. But this has no inherent or specific association with respect to an autistic human being.

Do autistic frequently people miss elements of social nuance? Yep.

Do autistic people focus so intently on a specific sensory experience, or on a complex thread of thought, that they might not notice you? Oh yeah!

Do autistic people speak too directly, or with painful honesty sometimes? Uh-huh.

I can't tell you how many times in my life that I have mis-read a room, or missed important social nuance in a situation, only to realize it a day, or even a week later. I have many times, found myself mortified when these situations finally unpack in my mind. Over the years, I've become familiar with cleaning up my messes. I don't get upset or beat myself up anymore. I just make the calls, write the notes, or make the apology or amends as called for.

But to say that autistic individuals have an **absence** of empathy is dehumanizing.

"Often obsess with efforts to express empathy, searching for clarity as to how empathy can best be expressed." is a much better take on this issue.

I will be reaching out to our friends at Merriam-Webster to begin a dialog on this issue. If you get there first, all the better. This can't be corrected soon enough.

Chapter 2

Hearts and Minds

I am reluctant to share this story. It involves a better moment of mine. For balance I should be providing a collection of my "worser" moments, but we don't have near enough time for all of that. I am sharing this story because I think it reflects a core tenant of this mission.

First, some background. When we received the autism diagnosis for TJ, I felt like it was going to be us against the world from that moment on. I wasn't sure what I should be doing, but I figured that somehow, I would need to become some sort of advocate warrior, doing battle with some sort of system, or something like that. For those old enough to remember, I probably watched the movie, Kramer v/s Kramer a few too many times.

It never occurred to me at that time, that most people truly yearn to love and to support people with cognitive differences, if only they have some idea how to do that.

Advocacy surely can have a place in all of this. Our kids depend on us to stand up for them. This means that we, as parents, will not hesitate to confront institutions or individuals who, intentionally or otherwise, are failing our kids.

I learned quickly that advocacy was about a lot more than conflict. When TJ was ten years old, I was asked to do a thirty-minute program on the topic of parent advocacy, on PBS Channel 9, here in St. Louis. During that program, my message was focused on solutions, rather than on complaining.

Fast forwarding to 2022, social media makes it really easy to get preachy, and to post guilt inducing memes. The autism message, as it stands today, often seems to place more energy on what is wrong with society instead of affirming what is right about autistic people. This is not a winning formula.

With all of this in mind, I want to share with you an incident that happened in Plano, Texas four years ago.

My son was involved in a road rage incident. A girl "brake checked" him hard; he could not stop in time; and he hit her.

At that time, I often traveled to Hong Kong and to Mainland China for work. I could easily have been on the other side of the planet, that afternoon, when that road rage incident happened.

Thankfully, I was in town and, I was in my car, about two miles away. TJ phoned me. He was upset and disoriented. He was having words with the other driver in the middle of a busy boulevard while we talked. The five minutes it took for me to get to the accident site felt like forever.

I was terrified that a responding officer might not read the situation well. We've all seen the stories about tragedies that have happened in similar circumstances.

An officer was already at the scene when I arrived. The cars had been moved out of traffic, into a nearby fire station parking lot. Generally speaking, things were okay. Everybody was safe. TJ was still really upset, but I was there, and we were ok.

TJ was charged as at fault for the accident. The reasoning was that since he was not able to avoid a car that was in front of him, then he did not have proper control of his car. I am pretty sure that a dash cam would have supported another verdict, but we did not have one in TJ's car.

All in all, I hated that it had happened, but more than anything else, I was overwhelmed with relief that my boy was okay. We could fix the car.

As the officer was finishing up the paperwork/citation, I walked over to the girl who had been driving the other car. I could see that she was tensing up. She probably thought I would be giving her a piece of my mind.

I said to her, "I'm sorry this happened and I'm glad nobody got hurt." I then said, "My son is autistic, and he can get really rattled by these sorts of situations."

As soon as I mentioned the word autistic, this girl, with a lot of tattoos and piercings, melted into tears. Through her tears, she told me she was very sorry.

I don't think that anybody would have blamed me for giving her a piece of my mind. But here's the thing, it wouldn't have helped. For one thing, by the way, I'm pretty sure that TJ had a part to play in this situation too. He can be an overly emotional driver, something that we continue to work on. Yelling at her just wouldn't have made planet earth a safer place for my son or for other autistic individuals.

I realize that sounds dramatic. It is just that, like most autism parents, I often think about what it will be like for my son, and for other autistic individuals, when I am no longer here.

She was only one person, with three other male passengers, all "tatted up" and pierced up just like her. They were all impacted in a good way that day. The world for autistic people wasn't radically changed, but it did get a little bit better, rather than a little bit worse.

Chapter 3

My Story

Just a quick intro for me so that you have some insight as to why I am writing this book.

I didn't receive my own mild autism diagnosis until my late 40's. That diagnosis helped me a lot to understand so many confusing events and experiences that have taken place throughout my life. A lot of those of those events had been haunting me for years. The diagnosis gave me permission to stop berating myself for many awkward and confusing events of the past. Now I can simply forgive myself instead.

Awkward and perplexing episodes, most involving social situations, had begun to occur a lot during my mid to late teens. Devastating anxiety attacks would consume me, every day, all day long when I was in high school. The anxiety attacks led to a suicidal depression.

By the time that I was in my early twenties, I was completely consumed in a vortex of suicidal depression. I had no hope for escape.

A series of miracles seemed to have materialized when I was twenty-one, and without expecting to, I found myself on a path to recovery. I began to meet with a really good therapist. It took several months before I began to trust her. Once that trust was established, she helped me to find hope again. With several more months of therapy work, I recovered from the anxiety attacks, and I began to emerge from the suicidal depression.

I was still pretty confused though. I still didn't understand that I was autistic. Things were better, but I didn't have a grasp on why I could be so clumsy and disoriented in social settings.

I began to lean more heavily on alcohol as my form of self-medication, eventually becoming a full-blown alcoholic. I entered into recovery in my early forties, and by God's grace, I remain sober and active in recovery to this day.

I had married at the age of twenty-eight. Mary, my wife an I had our first child, TJ, when I was twenty-nine years old. Courtney, our second child, was born a year and a half later.

Though much of my life up to that point had in many ways been searching and untethered. I found strength and clear purpose as a father.

I am, as it turns out, a huge empath. I believe that I was probably primed to be a strong advocate for my kids from the very beginning. TJ's autism diagnosis brought out my strength as a parent/advocate in ways that surprised me.

During TJ's early years, I was a territory sales representative and I traveled more than 50% of the time.

Elementary school came with its share of problems. When TJ was in the 1st grade, we agreed that I needed to get off the road. I resigned my sales position and we opened a printing, packing, and shipping business in a nearby town.

That business was successful, but we I sold it after three years. At that point, Mary and I had been in marriage counseling for a total of five years, and we had decided to divorce.

The retail business would not have allowed me the flexibility that I needed in order to work with TJ's teachers, the IEP team, etc., on daily issues.

After I sold the business, I began to work various jobs that would offer a flexible schedule. When TJ graduated high school, I returned to my former career as a sales manager, this time for a Kansas City based mini-bike and go-kart manufacturer. TJ and I moved from St. Louis to Kansas City for that job.

After seven years in Kansas City, TJ and I relocated to Plano, TX a suburb twenty minutes north of Dallas. There was an interesting tech program that had been created for young adult autistic people. It was located at the Plano campus of Southern Methodist University.

I accepted a new sales manager position, this time with a Hong Kong based toy manufacturer. That job allowed me to office at home. We had the flexibility to live anywhere in the United States.

I was making a decent income with the toy company, but TJ's tech program was expensive. In order to make ends meet, I began to do Uber rideshare driving on evenings and weekends when I was not traveling for work.

Little did I know that my ride share experience would lead to thousands of informal autism focus group conversations, and eventually to my new career as an author, TEDx speaker, conference speaker, and a Certified Special Needs Life Quality Coach.

It's funny how life works. I didn't expect for my journey to look anything like it does. Today I am finding more joy and passion from my work than I would ever have believed possible. I get to do work that I truly care about. I get to wake up each day in anticipation of lifting up and encouraging people from every walk of life.

I am deeply grateful.

Chapter 4

TJ's Story

I have apprehension about sharing both of our personal stories. I just don't believe that our experiences are any more relevant or any more important than are the countless stories of other autistic individuals and their families. But I feel like I have some obligation to let you in on who we are, where we've been, and how our experiences might have led us to a quest for greater societal connection.

TJ was born on March 21st, 1992. He had been meeting his common developmental milestones up until about the age of two. Between the ages of two and three, he became mostly non-verbal, but he would speak in great detail about cars, especially American Classic Muscle Cars!

He was also passionate about his Hot Wheels die cast car collection. He would spend hours meticulously lining up long rows of cars at perfect angles and with perfect spacing.

At first we thought that he may have been experiencing hearing loss. He seemed to be becoming less responsive to general noises.

Sometimes I would stand next to his bedroom door and whisper. Then I'd watch for a reaction. He did react to the whispers, so we could tell that his changes were not hearing related.

At around the age of three, TJ was diagnosed with a bone condition, multiple hereditary osteochondroma. This is a condition that both he and his sister Courtney, who was diagnosed two years later, had inherited from me.

As a child and adolescent, I had twelve corrective surgeries. TJ's first corrective bone surgery was scheduled when he was three. Ultimately, he had twenty-seven surgeries, and Courtney had twelve surgeries.

TJ also began attending early childhood development programs when he was three. We did not receive his official autism diagnosis from a neurologist until he was four.

Looking back, when TJ entered elementary school we were basically lost. We were trying to make sense of his IEP (Individual Education Plan), and how we were supposed to collaborate with the IEP Team of teachers, the behavior director, speech, and language therapists, and an Assistant Principle who attended every meeting. We had a parent advocate who helped, but to be honest, it seemed like she was speaking a foreign language too.

The primary focus of the IEP process centered around the idea of inclusion. TJ would begin the school day in a regular class, but as soon as he would act "differently", in a way that might disrupt the class, he would be removed from the class, and placed in the "cross-category" room

The cross-category room was a place where kids, usually kids with significant mental retardation, were kept. There were no organized educational activities in the cross-category room. The primary purpose of that room entailed knowing where those kids were and keeping them from escaping.

Autism was still a relatively new conversation in the mid 1990's. They didn't really have best practices or best approaches for autism. Everybody was pretty much winging it. Looking back, we were mostly missing the mark. We really didn't know what we didn't know.

One afternoon we got a call from the behavior director. An emergency IEP meeting had been called for the following day. We were told that TJ was having violent fantasies and that we had to discuss this issue right away.

As we waited for that meeting to begin, there were eight somber faces looking at us from across the table. Nobody said anything until the meeting began. I had no idea what we were about to hear. I had a sick feeling in my stomach.

As the meeting began, the behavior director described TJ's disturbing fascination with shotguns, and with shooting cars. Then somebody mentioned that TJ mentioned a shooting a radiator.

I breathed a big sigh of relief. One of TJ's favorite movies at that time was Disney's, *"The Fox and the Hound"*.

I described to them a scene in that movie where a nice old lady threatens to shoot the cantankerous old man's radiator out if he tried to harm the fox.

At that point, everybody understood. It was disturbing that the IEP Team reached such a dark conclusion about TJ so quickly. I could see how vulnerable TJ was in this process. I vowed in that moment to be a relentless advocate for him, to speak up anytime I would notice them misinterpreting or misunderstanding his behavior in any way. No detail would be too small to go unaddressed.

TJ spent most of his first-grade school year in that cross-category room. The behavior director told us that we should be prepared for institutionalization in his future. I him that I thought he was wrong.

We moved to another elementary school campus for his next four years of school. TJ was also assigned a one-on-one para-professional to assist him in the classroom.

The new school was better, but it was far from good. In many ways, we still didn't know what we didn't know. The cross-category room option was removed from his IEP plan. The behavior director at that school, did however, utilize a locked/padded room several times during TJ's first semester. That room was considered to be a "last alternative" when TJ would not "calm down" and "comply".

We put a stop to the padded room after a few of those episodes. TJ made some progress at the new elementary school, but he also became increasingly frustrated. The behavior director, nearing his retirement, operated on a belief that TJ was responsive to his "loud and booming voice".

By the end of his time at that elementary school, TJ had lost all patience with that guy. When sensory intensities are already enhanced, a loud voice is anything but calming and centering.

We looked for a fresh start as we moved on to middle school for his 6th grade school year.

The middle school behavior director and IEP team offered the promise of a more responsive, more informed and more effective approach.

It all sounded good, but eventually it became apparent that it was more of the same. I began to find myself at his school most days of the week. I would arrive at my work, get a phone call from the behavior director, and my workday would be over.

I could usually tell from the phone calls that the staff was misreading what was happening with TJ. Usually one "behavior problem" (misunderstanding) led to another, then to another, then another, etc.

I knew it would be too complicated to unpack all of that over the phone. It was just easier to go to the school, and to work with the staff to the extent that they would listen.

When I would arrive, the behavior director would want to deal with each of the "behavior problems" that had occurred that day. In practical terms, that would have been multiplying the sensory overload.

I learned to say to the behavior director and staff, "There comes a point when we are just lost in the woods. What matters now is to figure out how we walk out of the woods".

More times than not, I would take TJ home, and then we would come back with a fresh strategy for the next day.

I don't believe that the staff was being intentionally mean or malicious. They cared. There was just a whole lot that was not known or understood about autism two decades ago.

Special IEP team meetings were called with greater frequency. There was a continued focus on getting TJ to "comply", so that he could participate in their inclusion program.

But, they didn't actually have an inclusion program. They had a program that offered TJ an opportunity to deny his sensory realities, so that he could pretend to be like all the other kids.

Around this time, PBS Channel 9 in St Louis had come to the advocacy organization that we were working with, and they asked if there was a parent who would do a thirty-minute program about being an autism parent.

I was recommended, and I did the program. I brought with me, six bullet points to speak about. I addressed the idea that, given the rise in autism diagnosis, public schools should develop annex programs that are specifically designed to meet autistic kids at their place of sensory reality.

That PBS program was aired three times a day over the next month, and it went over well. At that time, I was a flat broke autism parent who didn't always have food or electricity, so I was in no position to support that sort of an initiative financially.

Today, many school systems are implementing programs similar to what I had proposed. In many ways, things are better for autistic students in public schools today. With the new, fundamental, and tangible information available today, I believe we can be confident that in general, things will continue to improve for autistic students.

Returning to TJ's story. He only understood that he was disappointing a lot of people, every day. He was becoming increasingly depressed.

I learned of a highly regarded therapeutic private school – The Logos School, located in the nearby suburb of Ladue, Missouri. I made an appointment to tour the school.

On the day of my tour, I walked into the small lobby of what was previously an abandoned elementary school. I checked in and sat down to wait for my tour guide.

As I waited, a really large and loud high school student walked into that small lobby. It was just him, me, and nobody else. He was yelling and cussing, and he was angry. I thought to myself, "Yikes!"

Then, I looked on as three school staff members approached him. Logos School always has staff "roamers" in the hall, plus a licensed therapist.

They began to process *with him*. They did not react *to him*. I thought, "Yes!! They just met that kid *where he is at!*" I desperately wanted for TJ to have that same experience, because, in the public school system, it had been quite a while since he had been met where he was at.

I toured the school that day, and I fell in love with it. They had a ratio of one licensed therapist, on site full time, for every eleven students. The students attended weekly individual therapy and weekly group therapy. The staff also provided real time processing with students throughout the day as situations arose. Most of that work would happen sitting on the steps outside of a classroom.

At the end of the tour, we visited the financial office. That is when I quickly returned to reality. Tuition was, at that time, $20,000 per year (35 K now). With all the trouble going on at TJ's school, I had been missing a lot of work. My finances were depleted, and I did not have the option to return to my career/income because of travel requirements.

As I drove home from Logos I was beating myself up. "Who do you think you are anyway? Visiting that rich people's school and wasting those people's time?"

Then, my cell phone rang. It was Mary calling to tell me that TJ had been sent home from school that day. We were following a 50/50 joint custody schedule at that time.

I asked why he was sent home. She told me that he said a cuss word. I said, "Big deal." And then she added that TJ would not stop talking about killing himself. He was eleven years old.

I drove to her house to pick up TJ, and we went out for an ice cream. As we were driving to McDonalds, TJ looked out the window. He said, "Dad?" I said," Yeah, what?". "If I am dead, will my friends divide my toys?". He wasn't contriving or being dramatic. He was being honest. My heart sank into my stomach.

We had ice cream and we talked. I felt like he was in a better mindset, at least temporarily, and then I drove him back over to Mary's.

On my way to my house my mind was racing. "I have to do something! But financially, I don't have the ability to do anything!"

After a few minutes of that, I stopped cold in my pacing. I thought to myself, "Money is not a good enough reason for TJ to not attend Logos School! It just isn't."

Then I sent an open email letter to our extended families. I wrote, "If you are currently involved in any philanthropic endeavors, we have an important project to consider that is very close to home."

My mother and my brother Olen stepped in with a great deal of financial help and we were also offered a scholarship from Logo's School for a portion of the tuition.

TJ attended Logos School for the next six years. From start to finish, Logos was an amazing place, and a great experience for TJ.

On a side note, I spoke to the behavior director at his public middle school before we made the move to Logos School. I told her all about Logos, the therapeutic environment and the successful outcomes that troubled students were finding there. She seemed genuinely excited about it.

To this point, I had believed that even though things were not going well, that she had truly been in our corner. So, I said to her, "I am glad that you are excited about this too! Will you recommend this program to the IEP Team?".

Sometimes, the IEP Team would approve support services outside of the school district for struggling students. But before I could finish that sentence, she was already responding, "Oh, God no!"

In that moment, I realized that her response was not personal. Her response was just an accurate reflection of school district culture and priorities. This had always been the case, but I was only realizing it in that moment.

After TJ attended Logos School for six years, he wanted to graduate from his local public high school. He left Logos and he did graduate from his public high school.

From a social standpoint, however, the public high school was not a positive experience. We basically endured until graduation. His closest friends to this day are his buddies from Logos School.

TJ had a successful full-time work experience immediately following his high school graduation in St Louis. Six months later we relocated to Kansas City

From TJ's standpoint, the move to Kansas City was a mixed bag at best. He bounced between a few jobs that never lived up to what was promised. He eventually settled into a job with a local grocery store chain, and he worked there for two and a half years.

The people centric nature of his job, the dirty reusable grocery bags that customers brought in, and the overall chaos of that situation began to take a toll on TJ.

Over time, he became stressed out, and he was slipping into a deep depression. We needed a change.

I had learned about an interesting program that was located in Plano, Texas called Non-Pareil Institute. This was a tech program for young adult autistic people. They built games and apps from scratch. They created the background scenes and did everything from game concept, coding, art, digital animation, etc... Each project would then be released for sale on iTunes.

We moved to Plano in November of 2015. TJ was successful in that program, but it did not really offer a legitimate path to career or income. TJ has always wanted to pursue his full independence, financially and otherwise. After a year and a half, we left that program.

He moved on to a job placement program with an excellent job coach. He landed a job working full time in light manufacturing. It was a good fit for him, working primarily with "stuff", and dealing less with people.

A year before Covid, TJ had a fall at work and fractured his hip. He had surgery to install pins and was in rehab for several months. He was just returning to full-time work when Covid happened. During Covid, in the fall of 2020, we moved back to St Louis so that TJ could be close to his school friends again.

He had been driving back to St Louis several times a year, while we were in Dallas, to spend weekends with his Logos School buddies. TJ never developed a social life in Dallas, so it made sense to come back to St. Louis. Now he spends most weekends with his friends.

TJ has a solid. well-paying job now in warehouse fulfillment. The company culture where he works is excellent, very supportive.

Long term, TJ and I plan to work together to acquire rental properties. The goal is to for us to have a portfolio of properties support both my retirement and his life for the long term.

TJ also wants to get involved in the American Classic Muscle Car community as an owner, buyer, and seller.

When TJ was in the first grade, we were very much feeling our way in the dark. It was scary to hear the "experts" say that he would likely be institutionalized. I rejected what said, but to be honest, I couldn't be sure of the future at that point. "Maybe they were right."

Today, TJ is thirty years old and quite not institutionalized. We have walked through many highs and of lows. The journey is far from over, and I can't wait for what comes next!

Chapter 5

A Twisted Path to the Autism Diagnosis

To understand our direction forward with the autism conversation, it is important to understand where we've been.

The official Autism diagnosis is quite young. As mentioned earlier, autism only became a recognized diagnosis in 1980. There are several key contributors who had notable influence that process.

Leo Kanner-(1894-1981), was an Austrian American psychiatrist. Kanner published his original research paper on autism titled, "Autistic Disturbances of Affective Contact" in 1943.

Kanner was born in Austria, educated in Berlin, and immigrated to the United States in 1924. He established the first children's psychiatric clinic in the United States at Johns Hopkins Hospital, Baltimore, MD in 1930.[7]

Kanner's original 1943 paper detailing his autism theory was largely on point. He coined the term, "infantile

---

[7] Ellen Herman, "LEO KANNER, 1894-1981," The Autism History Project, 2019, https://blogs.uoregon.edu/autismhistoryproject/people/leo-kanner-1894-1981/.

autism", asserting that autism was a condition largely present from birth.

Within that same paper, however, he referred to at least one set of parents as having increased the severity of their child's autism due to "cold parenting". The phrase "cold parenting" would later evolve to be explained as "refrigerator mothers".[8]

A Freudian influence was prevalent during this time. Sigmund Freud believed that most mental illness diagnoses could be attributed to emotional injury early in life.

In the years following his publication, Kanner began to move further away from his original primary assertion, that autism occurs at birth.

In 1949, he published a paper attributing the cause of autism to, "A genuine lack of parental warmth". Later, in a 1960 interview, Kanner described maternal parents of autistic children as having "Just happened to defrost enough to produce a child".[9]

I can't imagine the difficulty of being a parent of an autistic child during that time. Autism was not a well-

---

[8] Wikipedia, s.v. "Refrigerator Mother Theory," last modified January 23, 2022,
https://en.wikipedia.org/wiki/Refrigerator_mother_theory.
[9] Wikipedia, s.v. "Refrigerator Mother Theory."

known or recognized condition among society, and on top of that, most respected experts were placing the blame squarely on the parents.

Another early voice in the autism discussion was a German psychologist, Hans Asperger-(1906-1980). Asperger was the director of the University of Vienna Children's Clinic for most of his career.

While Asperger contributed to a greater understanding of autism, notably recognizing a broader spectrum (range of autism impact) than did Kanner, Asperger's past has some very dark chapters. He is an example that important societal contributions can sometimes come from people who have done evil things. As for Asperger, he participated in Nazi Germany programs that euthanized thousands of individuals who had cognitive differences, many of them autistic.[10]

The Cambridge University Press originally published His autism paper, **"'Autistic Psychopathy' in Childhood,** in

---

[10] Wikipedia, s.v. "History of Asperger Syndrome," last modified February 16, 2022,
https://en.wikipedia.org/wiki/History_of_Asperger_syndrome.

1944. His paper was translated into English and published by the Cambridge University Press in 1991.[11]

Asperger's specific research was first listed as an autism sub-type in the DSM in 1994.[12] (DSM – 5, released in 2014 has actually eliminated Asperger's as a sub-type of autism, and has rolled the Asperger's diagnosis into the Level 1 and Level 2 autism diagnosis.)[13]

Asperger could, by some measure, be seen as more of an early optimist regarding his views on autism. In addition to his assertion that the autism diagnosis has a broader spectrum of impact, he also asserted that autism is more widely prevalent among the general population.

In 1967, another influential, *at least temporarily*, contributor, Bruno Bettelheim injected himself into the autism conversation. Bettelheim was a popular, self-proclaimed psychologist who taught at the University of Chicago. He published his book titled *Empty Fortress: Infantile Autism and the Birth of Self* in 1972. Within this

---

[11] Ellen Herman, "HANS ASPERGER, '"AUTISTIC PSYCHOPATHY" IN CHILDHOOD,' 1944," The Autism History Project, 2019, https://blogs.uoregon.edu/autismhistoryproject/archive/hans-asperger-autistic-psychopathy-in-childhood-1944/.

[12] Herman, "Hans Asperger."

[13] American Psychiatric Association, *Diagnostic and Statistical Manual of Mental Disorders*, 5th ed. (Washington, D.C.: American Psychiatric Publishing, 2013).

book, Bettelheim compared autistic children to being in a concentration camp. He added that Autism kids were never given a chance to develop a personality. He also proclaimed, "Autism was the product of mothers who were cold, distant, and rejecting, thus depriving these children the chance to 'bond properly'".[14]

Bettelheim was publicly discredited as a plagiarist who vastly overstated his credentials in the mid 1970's, but still, great damage had been done.

This history, the good parts, and the very bad parts, serve as a baseline for understanding and for perspective. Mistakes were made in the past, to put it mildly. Many mistakes have been corrected with new and better information, and by better people who have confronted inexcusable wrongs of the past.

Good people, modern science, new and better ways of imaging, and excellent research are all working together to humanize the autism conversation.

New and better resources will continue to break down myths and perceived complexities about autism that have, in our past, served to inhibit true connection.

---

[14] Wikipedia, s.v. "Refrigerator Mother Theory."

Prior to DSM-5, there were more than 3,200 potential unique autism diagnosis.

DSM-5 has identifies three primary Autism Diagnosis:

Level 1 Autism - Mild Impact Autism.

Level 2 Autism - Moderate Impact Autism. Individuals who will have some independence in life, and who will also benefit from specific supports throughout life.

Level 3 Autism - High Impact Autism. These individuals will require significant living supports throughout life.[15]

---

[15] American Psychiatric Association, *Diagnostic and Statistical Manual of Mental Disorders*; Lisa Jo Rudy, "Understanding the Three Levels of Autism," Verywell Health, last modified October 30, 2021, https://www.verywellhealth.com/what-are-the-three-levels-of-autism-260233#level-3-requiring-very-substantial-support.

Chapter 6

Sensory Intensity Difference

A most fundamental definition for autism is *sensory intensity difference*. That's it. That's the story.

This fundamental definition is the first topic that I have sought to discuss with every expert that I have encountered over the past eight years.

The conversation usually goes something like this:

Me - "Am I missing something here?"

The response, universally, has been something like,

Expert - "No, you're not missing anything. This is on point."

Me - "So, then, this would be a really helpful concept for society to understand and embrace, right?"

Expert - "Yes!"

Me - "Cool!"

Of course, autism manifests uniquely with each autistic individual, but understanding each individual by unique personality attributes is something that we have always described as, "getting to know a person!" We don't need to be a neurologist to do this!

Complexity dehumanizes. Simplicity humanizes. If this is true, and I am convinced that it is, then *sensory intensity difference* is a fundamental definition that anybody can embrace and internalize.

So many times, as I speak with people in the general public, well-intentioned people to be sure, I will at some point hear something like, "You know, to be honest, there is just so much that I don't know about autism." This is a common misperception. One that can be easily cleared up.

We hear a lot about the term "Spectrum". It sounds complicated and daunting. But the term, "spectrum", relative to the autism conversation, simply informs that each autistic person is unique. Again, should we be surprised by this?

I don't minimize the unique sensory challenges that are an important part of navigating planet earth for autistic individuals.

Sensory experiences that involve greater intensities have predictable impacts. Legitimate impacts to be sure. But again, these effects can be simple to grasp at a fundamental level!

When we can understand sensory intensity differences at a fundamental level, then we are no longer compelled to tighten up when we encounter autistic people. No need to walk on eggshells. We can warm up and connect instead! Rather than to step back, we can lean in. We can interact and collaborate with each individual at the level of connection that they are comfortable with. We can humanize each encounter.

As I have researched this project, I have been haunted by one issue. How will this mission, and this message, be received by autism level-3 families? A message that is relentlessly optimistic, even celebratory?

I have personally spoken with many Level-3 autism families about this concern. I will always ask the same question, "Does your autistic loved one move toward the people who are comfortable with them?". The response is always the same, "Yes, absolutely!".

I have needed to know this because these are the autism families whose lives are most impacted by autism. I needed to know that there is something in this message that will love, lift up, support, and encourage autism Level-3 families too.

For the Level-1 and Level-2 autistic individuals, a society that has more understanding people, employers, law enforcement personnel, service providers, etc., this opens the way for greater societal opportunities, and greater opportunities for friendships and for relationships.

And for Level 3 autistic individuals, we can be confident in our support and in our fundamental understanding. Even when there are no obvious or apparent signs of communication or connection, even then, we can embrace the whole and complete dignity of that person. We can enter that space with them. We can project warmth and safety.

Chapter 7

Physical-Tangible-Logical

As I mentioned earlier, I spoke with Temple Grandin at Autism conferences in Dallas on two occasions. Once in September of 2018, and again in September of 2019.

For those not familiar, Temple Grandin is the first widely known public figure diagnosed as autistic. Temple was non-verbal until the age of four, yet she would go on to be recognized as one of the Top 100 Most Influential Women in the World.

Born in 1947, only four years after the original Autism paper was published, Temple was born into a society that had no knowledge or concept of autism.

It was normal, even expected, that kids with cognitive differences, like Temple, would be handed over to a state institution, where she would have been essentially warehoused for life.

Temple's mother, Anna Eustacia Purves (now Cutler). Anna was the daughter of John Coleman Purves, (co-inventor of the auto-pilot aviation system). Anna stubbornly rejected the medical establishment recommendation that Temple should be institutionalized.

Anna also faced intense pressure from her husband, Dick Grandin. He wanted to send their daughter away. Dick Grandin went as far as to keep secret notes on Anna for a period of three years. He then took those notes to a psychiatrist and attempted to have Anna committed for insanity. When Anna learned of this, she promptly divorced him.

Anna had no medical advisors or therapists to guide her, but she had great instincts. She never lost focus of Temple as a whole and complete person. She paid close attention to what most interested Temple, and she consistently exposed Temple to new activities.

They lived on a working cattle farm. Temple developed a strong interest in the cattle/beef processing operations. During high school, Temple's science teacher took notice, and he arranged for her to spend one day of each week away from school, on site, observing and studying a cattle processing operation.

Temple would sometimes place herself in the cattle squeezers, machines that would hold the cows still during the milking process. She found that the deep pressure was soothing and comforting for sensory overstimulation.

With that in mind, she redesigned a squeeze machine so that it would fit a human body. Deep pressure therapy utilizing these types of machines, and weighted blankets, has become standard, effective, and commonly applied therapies today.

Temple also paid close attention to the cattle handling facilities, taking note of the stress that the animals would experience during that process.

She created a revolutionary redesigned cattle handling facility that would replace all hard-angled chutes with rounded and flowing chutes. She got down on her hands and knees and crawled through the chutes, making note of every object or element within her direct or peripheral vision that might startle or spook an animal.

Temple created meticulous, complex, and perfect to scale architectural renderings for her new concept design. This is significant because Temple had no training in architectural drawing.

Today in America, more than half of the cattle processing facilities in operation have been designed by Temple. She has also been called upon by numerous international companies to re-design their cattle handling operations.

As the public face of autism, for decades, several research organizations have requested periodic access to study Temple's brain development through MRI scans.

In 1991, a new technology was introduced. Functional MRI (fMRI). This process is also described as Realtime MRI.

With fMRI, static images become live images that reveal brain synapse firing in real time.

This fMRI was used to examine Temples brain, and when observing the region of her brain that processes spatial/object recognition, the visual tract, an fMRI scan reveals 400% overdevelopment of sensory processing material (white matter). This area of the brain is highly engaged and relied upon when doing the work of architectural rendering.

Another significant revelation is that Temple has a deficit of white matter in the specific portion of her brain activated with speech processing, the "say what you see" region of the brain. She has 1% of typical white matter development in this region. This helps to explain why Temple was non-verbal until the age of four, and why she struggled with a tic similar to stuttering as she was learning how to speak.

To better understand fMRI, in Temple's book, *The Autistic Brain*, she shares, "It is important to note that the neuroimaging provided by fMRI does not provide identical detail each time the brain is scanned"

The fMRI does not produce 3-D images of the brain. Instead, as neurons fire within a specific area of the brain, it will appear a lot like a lightning storm. The synapse event will begin with a glow, then the area will light up to a peak of brightness, and then the synapse will fade to dark.

The fMRI observes these brain responses as a patient lies still. While the fMRI does not capture a three-dimensional image, it certainly provides evidence that autism is present, physically, within the brain. This is significant in confirming that autism is tangible. The fMRI confirms that autistic behaviors are not just understandable, autistic sensory intensity experiences are physical, logical, therefore not optional.

I speak with autism moms from many different countries, and from many ethnic communities within the US. One young mother shared with me about her family members who would implore her to "make that kid act right!".

When you think about it, if autism sensory intensity experiences are in fact, physical, logical, and not optional, then by every reasonable consideration, that kid actually **is** acting right! The behaviors represent completely logical responses to legitimate sensory experiences.

This is not to say that sensory responses and behaviors that might impede opportunities and general life quality should not be addressed through therapies or other beneficial strategies. That is not the point.

The point goes back to our current we/they societal mindsets about individuals with cognitive differences. With better information, we as a society can shift that paradigm. We can do so much better.

And when we do, the prospects for advanced and enhanced life experience on are beyond measure. And that is truly exciting!

I recently spoke with a neuro-science grad student at Washington University in St Louis. He explained to me that not only does autism have a physical signature within the human brain, but that all cognitive differences have a physical signature within the human brain. This includes diagnoses like ADD, ADHD, OCD, and even depression.

He noted that instruments have not yet been developed yet that can measure every brain anomaly associated with a diagnosis, but that we know, at least theoretically, that every cognitive difference will have a physical representation within the brain.

There are also newer developing MRI technologies that measure brain function by assessing the direction of water diffusion (water molecules rush to certain areas of the brain when activated for processing).[16] There is an even

---

[16] Rebecca Schmidt et al., "Highly Shifted Proton MR Imaging: Cell Tracking by Using Direct Detection of Paramagnetic Compounds," *Radiology* 272, no. 3 (August 2014): 615-7,

more a recent technology, developed in 2018, that measures the calcium content present in specific processing areas of the brain.[17]

These newer techniques provide greater detail in brain flow and in function. The calcium MRI measurements are providing detailed views that go much deeper into the brain.

I often speak with parents or with family members of an autistic individual who want to avoid the perception of stigma that they associate with an autism diagnosis.

As this physical evidence within the brain, both simple to understand and profound in relevance, becomes more widely understood, any hesitancy to pursue, to accept, and to embrace autism wholly and completely can only be seen as denial.

---

https://doi.org/10.1148/radiol.14132056; Terisa P. Gabrielsen et al., "Functional MRI Connectivity of Children With Autism and Low Verbal and Cognitive Performance." *Molecular Autism* 9, no. 67 (2018). https://doi.org/10.1186/s13229-018-0248-y; Rong Chen, Yun Jiao, and Edward H. Herskovits, "Structural MRI in Autism Spectrum Disorder," *Pediatric Research* 69, (2011): 63-8, https://doi.org/10.1203/PDR.0b013e318212c2b3.

[17] Anne Trafton, "Calcium-based MRI Sensor Enables More Sensitive Brain Imaging," MIT News, April 30, 2018, https://news.mit.edu/2018/calcium-based-mri-sensor-enables-more-sensitive-brain-imaging-0430.

There is reason for hope when an autism diagnosis is revealed. The brain is malleable. Neural pathways are capable of some change. These pathways can re-develop to a measurable degree with the implementation of therapeutic programs and exercises.

Therapies and treatments can and do benefit individuals who are on the autism spectrum in the same way that physical therapy can benefit an athlete who is seeking to maximize performance.

But there is a fine line that we should always recognize. The line that separates the ideal of growth versus the ideal of acceptance. Pushing any individual towards their highest potential is love in action. Placing a desire for growth ahead of acceptance is getting the cart before the horse. It's an easy thing to do. I don't judge. I have been there, and I have done that too.

What I have learned on my autism journey with TJ is that the discipline to accept is always more important than the desire for growth. Equipped with the power of acceptance, we can lock arms to seek out the best programs and therapies. We can grow together.

https://stm.sciencemag.org/content/9/393/eaag2882?platform=hootsuite

Chapter 8

Whole and Complete

Knock-knock.

Who's there?

Me.

Me who?

Me - Me! Who else did you think would be in here?

I was involved in several autism parent support groups during the early years, after having received TJ's autism diagnosis. I was also a member of a committee in St Louis that was responsible for raising funds for an organization called The National Association of Autism Research (NAAR).

NAAR was formed in 1994. The NAAR organization placed a shared emphasis on the acceptance of the autistic individual, and on autism research.

Our local St. Louis NAAR committee would organize and manage a large fundraiser walk that would take place each fall in St Louis. These fundraisers were well attended, and we raised a lot of money.

Then a new group named Autism Speaks was formed in February of 1995.[18] This organization had celebrity influence, high visibility, and strong financial support.

At the time of its formation and for many years after, Autism Speaks was intensely focused on a Hallmark story scenario where autism is cured and eradicated.

In 1996, Autism Speaks and NAAR national leaderships decided to merge organizations. They believed that their combined resources and experience would benefit the overall agendas of research, acceptance, and *cure*. Within this new arrangement, Autism Speaks was positioned as the parent umbrella entity.

When this merger happened, I stepped out of the picture. I just couldn't be a part of it.

After I ended my affiliation with NAAR, I cranked up my AOL internet modem, and I began to search. I was hoping to find other people or organizations that shared my stubborn position on the obsession with cure. With that, I found an on-line organization based in NYC called GRASP.

---

[18] *Autism Speaks officially removed the word cure from their mission statement and from all organizational media in September of 2014. Good on them for doing so.*

GRASP is short for Global and Regional Asperger Syndrome Partnership. As of this writing, it has long been the largest support organization created by and run by adults who are on the autism spectrum.

The leader of the organization at that time was a guy named Michael Jon Carley. He was a Broadway playwright. His son had been diagnosed on the spectrum in late 2000, and then Michael, too, was diagnosed one week later.

What compelled me the most when I read about the GRASP organization was their mission statement. It was actually radical at that time. To paraphrase, it said something like, "Stop trying to cure us. We're not sick! And, by the way, we like ourselves the way we are!"

I connected with Michael on a phone call. I was relieved to speak with another person who shared my view on the cure issue.

GRASP had several chapters, and an active website that included several excellent autistic writers. One of those writers was a girl named Amanda. Amanda had been significantly impacted by her autism. Throughout her childhood and adolescence, she found her comfort in life mostly through stimming in a corner, alone.

At that time, people, even those closest to her, had doubted her intellectual capacity. Because of her stimming and her lack of engagement with those around her, it was believed that she had little or no intellectual capacity.

As a young adult, as Amanda began to write, she didn't just write technically well. Her writing also connected powerfully on every level of emotion.

In other words, Amanda was a whole and complete person, emotionally, spiritually, and intellectually. And... she always had been. Even when those closest to her doubted this.

The takeaway that I hope we will find here is that whenever we encounter an autistic person, regardless of their level of autistic sensory impact, we can know that person is whole, and complete, on every level, in every way, every time, no exceptions. And that this is never not true.

Chapter 9

Be Right There!

One of the daily battles that I fought with the public school system IEP team back in the early days had to do with TJ "not following directions!".

I would have taken them at their word that this was a problem except that TJ followed every direction I gave him at home. As a little guy, he was remarkably compliant with me.

Alas, today, he is a thirty-year-old dude with an impressive stubborn streak reminiscent of his dad's stubborn streak. As it should be. I love to watch him grow in his identity and his independence. At some point, he will need to do this life without me. I am increasingly assured, he'll be up to the job.

Back to our "failure to comply" story. At home, I would give TJ a ten-minute heads up, a five-minute reminder, and a one-minute alert for any upcoming transition. By doing that, TJ moved effortlessly from one task or activity to the next. How come?

We now know that sensory experiences of autistic individuals can be fifty to one-hundred times of greater intensity relative to those same sensory experiences for the general population.

This is true for touch, taste, smell, sound, and sight. And when you consider people like Einstein, Nikola Tesla, Mozart, Michelangelo, Steve Jobs, Elon Musk, etc., the intensity of thought processing has to be a part of this conversation, too.

If an average person might go two, three, or four corridors deep into connecting thoughts about a main topic, isn't it logical to assume that an autistic person might go twenty, thirty or fifty corridors deep into connecting thoughts?

When teachers would, without warning say to TJ, "OK, time to stop doing this, now let's do that!", this was, in practical consideration, an unfair, even impossible request.

The problem is that TJ was not "here", he was "there", down those numerous corridors of thought at that moment of interruption.

Providing him with time prompts allows for him to work his way back through all of those connecting corridors of thought, back to the here and now. This is a topic that I have discussed with hundreds of experts over these past six years. This description, supported by science and by logic, has been affirmed by all of them.

This issue with TJ and the IEP Team all came to a head during the middle of his sixth-grade school year. During every IEP meeting, and at this point, and there were a lot of them, I would hear again and again from the staff and specialists that TJ was "non-compliant!".

From TJ's perspective, he only saw the long faces, the frustrated faces, the faces of disapproval. TJ has a beautiful and kind heart. He desperately wanted to please others, and from his perspective, he was failing them miserably, seemingly with no hope for change.

It was at this point that he became suicidal, and the situation was only getting worse. That is when through family support and through grants, I found a way to remove him from the public school system.

It is really important to see the ramifications of blaming an autistic kid for doing nothing more than living his or her legitimate life/sensory experiences.

Along those lines, when an autistic loved one speaks of suicidal ideation, our first response has to be to believe them, and then to do whatever it takes.

A large study conducted in December 2015 by the Karolinska Institute in Stockholm, Sweden, utilizing their National Patient Registry, found that individuals with mild autism are ten times more likely to die of suicide than those of the general public.[19]

[19] Ann Griswold, "Large Swedish Study Ties Autism to Early Death," Spectrum News, December 11, 2015, https://www.spectrumnews.org/news/large-swedish-study-ties-autism-to-early-death/.

Chapter 10

Cure or Acceptance

For many years I held a singular view about the autism cure movement, namely that it is completely intolerable.

About five-years ago, I was speaking with a young lady who had recently relocated from Chicago to North Dallas. We were, of course, discussing autism topics. I was sharing with her my issues related to the autism cure movement.

"Cure sounds like eugenics to autistic people!"; "We like ourselves just the way we are!", "We don't want a cure!". I was expecting her to be nodding along with me on all of this, but that is not what happened.

She replied, "Actually, I think there is a solid case to be made for the cure movement."

She told me about a close friend, one who has a child that is Level-3 autistic. She said, "This child will never be independent, and this child will always require extensive supports. Wouldn't it be better if this child, and this family, had a different life?"

This issue had, of course, been haunting me throughout the process of writing this book, but I had been trying to ignore it.

I attempted to defend my position with her. I talked about the many gifts to humanity that every autistic human soul has to offer. I talked about the inherent dignity of every living being. I talked about the incredible inventions that have emerged from within the autism community, and anything else that I could think of.

She didn't budge. "I get all of that, but, again, wouldn't advances in science and in medicine be a good thing? Wouldn't it be better if my friend's son had the chance to live a full and complete life just like other kids?"

I couldn't deny that she was making good points, but still, I thought, "I can't give in!"

And then... I surrendered.

Above all else, I trust in God's plan. I have a hard time imagining life without autistic people as an important, essential part of our humanity. But if it would ever be God's plan for autism to be eradicated from life as we know it, then I trust that God would be taking us to a better place. I am just clear, that for me, this is not a part of my mission. I don't think it ever will be.

That encounter was helpful for me though. It pushed me to think through a problem that I had been hiding from. I found a greater perspective and greater clarity about the specific direction of this mission. And for that, I am deeply grateful

Chapter 11

Undeniable

I was speaking with an affluent father once who began to describe his son to me. He talked about the possibility that his son might be autistic. He described traits and behaviors to me that shouted autism. He also shared with me that his son had not seen a neurologist. They had no diagnosis.

I became excited for this father and for his son. From personal experience, I know that for an autistic person, newfound clarity, and acceptance, especially from loved ones, is a big deal. It is a process of emerging from disorienting uncertainty. To be seen, fully recognized, and to experience approval. I encouraged that father to seek out the insight that a full evaluation would provide.

It was at this point in our conversation that he interrupted me and said, "You know, my son is actually doing pretty well without all of that diagnosis and labeling stuff. I think were gonna just keep doing what we are doing. We will just continue to work through this."

Unfortunately, for those who are autistic, working through this is not an option. His son might be confused by many things in his life, but I can assure you, there is one thing that he is not confused about. That, on some level, he is letting his father down. On some level, he is not measuring up. On some level, he is not enough. And of course, he's blaming it all on himself.

When we view fMRI images and we see the physical evidence of autism in the brain, then we understand very well that "working through this" is not actually an option for that boy.

That boy will probably continue pretending to be something other than who he really is. He will try to please his father. He will deny himself in that process.

If you think about it, this actually goes beyond a fathers denial. This is rejection of what is real and tangible.

When we take our kids to a doctor, we want that doctor to tell us everything, right? We want to know every attribute of our kids from head to toe. Of course we do.

Yet, somehow, when it comes to comes to cognitive differences like autism, often times people will view these issues as optional. Cognitive differences are, of course, not optional. Cognitive differences are also not inherently negative.

I know that this this father loves for his son. I just pray that he keeps thinking about our conversation, and that he will be moved to seek real answers, real insights about who his son truly is.

Chapter 12

Fuzzy Animal Encounter

Acceptance looks so much better.

I'd like to share another encounter that I had while driving for Uber in Dallas. I picked up a mother and daughter at Love Field, they had flown in from Houston for the weekend to attend something called a "Furry Animal Convention".

Furry Conventions, new to me, apparently take place in several cities throughout the US each year. Kids and adults wear full size, elaborate fuzzy animal costumes, get together, and have fun! That's my take anyway.

The girl started to tell me about the convention right away. I she was really excited, and quirky, in a pleasant way. Mom seemed just along for the ride. She was warm and supportive of her daughter.

Mom asked me about driving for Uber. I explained that TJ and I moved to Dallas for an autism program and that I started driving part-time for extra money about four years earlier. I told her about my autism project, how the extra money was helping to make it all possible.

With my mention of autism, she started to tell me about her eight-year-old son. She said that some of his behaviors and expressions seemed autistic in nature.

She went on to say, that honestly, she thought that he was probably autistic. She told me that the school system had been pressuring her to get him tested for years, but she had been resisting.

She told me she was reluctant to do the testing because she didn't want the school system to "hang a label on him".

She asked me what I thought about all of that. I asked her, "Can I be direct?". She said, "Yes, please", and I could tell that she meant it.

So, I told her, "I realize that this may sound harsh, but autism is not an option for him. But, if he feels like you want him to not have Autism, then he will pretend, to the best of his ability, to not have autism. In doing so, he will be pretending to be somebody other than who he really is."

I went on to say, "For somebody who is on the autism spectrum, getting a diagnosis is actually a relief. Personal struggles and failures begin to make sense with a confirmed diagnosis. We begin to forgive ourselves".

She seemed to exhale a little bit, and she quietly said, "I get it". I could see that she really did get it.

The next part of this encounter might sound like a script that I wrote, but I promise, I didn't.

The daughter started to speak. She said, "Mom, you know that I am autistic too". And mom slowly nodded.

The daughter went on to say, in a kind way to her mom, "I really wish I had been diagnosed a long time ago. I beat myself up for a lot because I didn't understand why I was like I was". "I figured it out myself by googling information and articles about autism. I just wish that I had known sooner".

Mom was moved. She pieced together a sentence that went something like, "This is a lot, this will change things".

I was so incredibly happy. I was glad that the daughter was able to break through with her mother. I was also so happy for that little guy back in Houston.

Acceptance is to be seen. Glorious!

Chapter 13

The Indispensable Role of Autism in Society

Often, I will hear people say things like, *"You know, some of those autistic people are really smart!"*. I ponder to myself, "Ya think?!".

These comments often come across as surprising realizations that are spoken in hushed tones. "My friends' autistic daughter is really smart! I mean, seriously, I'm not kidding!"

I truly believe that as people become more familiar with fundamental understandings about autism, that these sorts of "epiphanies" will be retired and will be replaced with logical affirmations instead.

The irony is that modern civilization is in many important ways, only modern thanks to brilliant autistic visionaries. Many are deservedly famous. Countless other autistic creators and innovators are nameless, quietly making important improvements that seamlessly flow into our daily lives.

I will list out many of the famous inventors and innovators blow. Keep in mind this list only scratches the surface, but it is an amazing list, nonetheless.

The next time somebody wants to patronize your autistic child, sibling, loved one, or acquaintance, we can kindly remind them that this person might well be the next world changer. Act accordingly!

Scientific Discoveries

- **Benjamin Franklin** – Electricity.
- **Thomas Edison** – Electric lighting.
- **Albert Einstein** – Theories of Light, Gravity, and Energy.
- **Nikola Tesla** – Alternating Electric Current.
- **Bill Gates** – Intuitive Computer Operating Systems.
- **Steve Jobs** – Smart phone technology.
- **Sir Isaac Newton** -Three Laws of Motion.

Livestock Management

- **Temple Grandin**
  - Humane redesign of cattle handling facilities. More than ½ of the current facilities in America are designed by Temple.
  - Recognized as one of the Top 100 most influential women in the world.

Music

- **Wolfgang Amadeus Mozart**
  - Music composer of the Classical period
- **Bob Dylon** - Folk music legend.
- **David Byrne** - New wave music pioneer.

Art

- **Michaelangelo** - Italian painter, sculptor, painters, and architect.   His achievements include Sistine Chapel frescoes.
- **Vincent Van Gogh** - Dutch post-impressionist painter. Works include "A Starry Night".
- **Andy Warhol** - American modern pop art pioneer.

Literature

- **Emily Dickenson** - Poet.
- **Hans Christian Anderson** - Danish author best remembered for his fairy tales, including "The Little Mermaid" and "The Ugly Duckling."

Entertainment - Producers

- **Stanley Kubric** - *The Shining*.
- **Tim Burton** - *Edward Scissorhands*
- **Steven Spielburg** - *E.T.*

Entertainment - Actors

- Sir Anthony Hopkins - *Silence of the Lambs*
- Dan Akroyd - *Ghostbusters*
- Darryl Hannah - *Fish*

"You know, some of those autistic people are really smart!"

Facts!

Chapter 14

Common Sounds

When we think about sensory experiences in the abstract, it's hard to have a clear picture of what autistic sensory experiences are really like.

With that in mind, specific to hearing, following is a list of common sound references.

When we consider that autistic individuals might hear these sounds at potentially 50 to 100 times greater intensity, then it becomes clear why autistic people will sometimes prefer **not** to do some of the things that normies like to do. Maybe things like going to loud venues, a hockey game, a loud concert, a bustling city street, etc.

Of course this concept applies to other senses, a smelly fish market, clothes with scratchy tags, fluorescent lighting, etc...

In the same way that you may enjoy being in these places, an autistic individual can equally appreciate **not** being in these places. We're not missing out, we're actually right where we want to be, right where we like to be.

When we get this, we simply accept individual preferences for what they are. Not good, not bad, just different.

With this in mind, here are some common sound measurement references. These sound ratings are based on normal hearing measurements.

Imagine 30 or 50 times greater intensities.

130db - Jet engine at 100 ft.

120db - Thunder - *Pain Threshold Level*

110 db - Rock Music, Screaming Child.

90 db - Factory Machinery at 3 ft.

80 db - Busy Street, Alarm Clock

70 db - Busy Traffic, Phone Ringtone

60 db - Normal Conversation at 3 ft.

50 db - Quiet Office, Quiet Street

40 db - Quiet Residential Park

30 db - Quiet Whisper at 3 ft., Library

20 db - Rustling Leaves, Ticking Watch

Chapter 15

The Workplace

Sometimes I attend support group meetings for adults who are diagnosed on the spectrum.

I recently spoke with a friend at one of those meetings about her job situation. She is twenty-seven years old and married.

She is a research biologist by training, however, after entering that field of work, she realized that the work she really wants to do is to code writing.

She discussed this with her husband and he fully supported her in leaving her research position to take an entry level position as a coder.

As a coder, she currently works for an upstart tech company, one that has an open office format to encourage collaboration. On most days she finds the open office environment to be highly distracting.

She told me that there are days when she can block out all of the activity around her. On those days, she gets locked in and she gets a lot of work done. On those days, it might be 6:30 or 7:00 in the evening before she will realize it.

But she told me that her manager has no idea how much happier she would be if she could be permitted to work in a basement, in a corner, alone, most of the time.

She's not going to say anything though. She is entry level and she doesn't want to cause trouble. Her plan is to get needed experience at this company, and then she will search out a new work environment that will better suit her.

She is smart, motivated, passionate, talented, yet her current company will probably lose her, and they will probably never even know why.

When companies begin to instinctively run toward and embrace differences, rather than to incentivise and reward uniformity, the upside can be huge!

Chapter 16

The Opportunity!

The rate of ASD diagnosis in the United States is estimated by the CDC as of 2022 to be one in forty-four.[20]. As a rounded number, this amounts to .028 of our population.

One significant point to consider here is that one in forty-four actually falls within the range of what is considered to be statistically *normal.*

According to USAFACTS, The USA population as of May 2023 is 332.6 million.[21]

By applying those numbers as a baseline, then the USA population represented on the autism spectrum will equal 9,312,800 persons.

It is estimated that 65% of individuals on the autism spectrum are classified within the Level-1 and-2. categories. These are individuals who are capable and available for participation and contribution to the workforce.

---

[20] "Autism Spectrum Disorder (ASD) Data & Statistics," Centers for Disease Control and Prevention, December 2, 2021, https://www.cdc.gov/ncbddd/autism/data.html.
[21] " https://www.census.gov/popclock/ "

65% of our autistic Level-1 and Level-2 population within the USA equals **6,053,320** individuals.

Current estimates are that 90% of these individuals who are Level-1 and Level-2 autistic, available for work, are unemployed or underemployed.

That 90% number **amounts to 5,447,988 of Level-1 and Level-2** individuals who are unemployed or under-employed.

Without repeating all of those numbers again, and by narrowing down our reference to the Dallas-Fort Worth metro area population, these same calculations reveal that there are **83,896 Level-1 and Level-2** individuals in DFW alone who are unemployed or underemployed. 83,896![22] Does that number excite you as much as it excites me? The untapped and available potential is truly beyond measure.

I recently spoke with a venture capitalist who is also an adjunct professor at Columbia University in New York. We were talking about the difficulties that employers are currently experiencing in finding employees.

---

[22] Wikipedia, s.v. "Dallas-Fort Worth Metroplex," last modified February 9, 2022, https://en.wikipedia.org/wiki/Dallas%E2%80%93Fort_Worth_metroplex.

He shared with me that he had just done a presentation to a large conference on this topic.

His angle is that back in the 1950's, there was a ratio of approximately 7.5 workers to each retired person. Today, that number is less than 2.5 workers, and the United States just experienced a net zero-population growth rate. That means zero people to replace those who retire.

With that in mind, the idea of bringing more autistic talent into the workplace begins to really make sense from a purely practical perspective.

Chapter 17

It's Us!

One of my coping tricks for navigating social situations is to *keep my foot on the brake*. What I mean by that is, left unchecked, I will generally go four levels deeper into any topic of conversation than most other human beings had ever hoped to go, unless "I keep my foot on the brake". I can't say that I am always successful with this, not by a long shot, but of course, I keep on trying.

I am not able to fully express how excited I am about a movement to simplify, and to humanize the autism conversation. To promote more profound human connections, and on a larger scale, to promote greater authentic connection relative to every cognitive difference.

That said, I fear that from the perspective of those not on the autism spectrum, that this could all sound like minor tweaks, polishing the edges, rather than this all-encompassing, humanizing shift in perception that we on the spectrum yearn for.

It is easier to communicate radical changes. Effectively communicating nuanced changes takes more intentionality and more work.

But then again, the more that I think about it, we're really not talking about nuanced changes here are we? We really are talking about radical change. We are talking about redefining the fundamental way that our society views and contextualizes cognitive differences like autism. In other words, a paradigm shift not unlike the 1930's shift away from systemic institutionalization.

I have spoken with so many people who are like me. People who have been in this autism game for a long time. We have been there to meet the 24/7 challenges. So anytime it begins to feel like somebody might be trying to re-frame my story in any way, truth be told, I don't instinctively react well.

We are the warriors for our loved ones. We are also, in many ways, understandably protective of our narratives. I pray that I will always remain searching and teachable, and that as a community, and as a society, we will strive to remain searching and teachable too.

We shifted away from those 1930's "best practices" because new and better information became available, known and accepted.

Today, we know more about autism. A lot more. Today we know that autism is physical and tangible, visible within the human brain. We know that autistic enhanced sensory experiences are not optional, they are logical. Not good, not bad, just a different kind of different.

Today we understand that there are not endless types of autism, there is one. Sensory intensity difference. There are of course infinite levels of impact.

Today, we know that while the term spectrum may sound daunting and complex, in actuality the term spectrum only serves to state the obvious, that each autistic human being is unique

Even with all that we know, the science of human anatomy is impossibly complex. There are so many unanswered questions. Science is important, really important, but not most important. Humanity comes first! We will always yearn to be known, embraced, and accepted for precisely who we are, right here, right now, in this moment.

This all-in acceptance has to be our highest priority. The beginning mindset for each day, for each encounter, for each appointment, etc.. And then, from that sacred place of honest acceptance, we are empowered seek out the therapies, treatments, and educational opportunities that will spur growth, joy, and greater life quality.

All human beings have anomalies and imperfections. All anomalies and imperfections are valid and legitimate.

The We/they dynamic represents a false ideal.

It's us!

It always has been.

Thank you for reading my book.

I would deeply appreciate it if you will take a minute to rate and add a comment on Amazon.

Ratings are the most effective way for this book to be found by others who are searching for encouraging, life affirming, and hopeful information about autism.

If you have further questions, or would like to connect please feel free to reach me via email at:
Tony@autismsimplified.org

For more information about scheduling speaking engagements, please visit my website.
www.autismsimplified.org

Bibliography

American Psychiatric Association. *Diagnostic and Statistical Manual of Mental Disorders*. 5th ed. Washington, D.C.: American Psychiatric Publishing, 2013.

Centers for Disease Control and Prevention. "Autism Spectrum Disorder (ASD) Data & Statistics." December 2, 2021. https://www.cdc.gov/ncbddd/autism/data.html.

Chen, Rong, Yun Jiao, and Edward H. Herskovits. "Structural MRI in Autism Spectrum Disorder." *Pediatric Research* 69, (2011): 63-8. https://doi.org/10.1203/PDR.0b013e318212c2b3.

DeNoon, Daniel J., "Autism Improves in Adulthood." WebMD. September 27, 2007. https://www.webmd.com/brain/autism/news/20070927/autism-improves-in-adulthood.

Emerson, Robert W., Chloe Adams, Tomoyuki Nishino, Heather Cody Hazlett, Jason J. Wolff, Lonni Zwaigenbaum, John N. Constantino, et al. "Functional Neuroimaging of High-Risk 6-Month-Old Infants Predicts a Diagnosis of Autism At 24 Months of Age." *Science Translational Medicine* 9, no. 393 (June 2017). https://doi.org/10.1126/scitranslmed.aag2882.

Gabrielsen, Terisa P., Jeff S. Anderson, Kevin G. Stephenson, Jonathan Beck, Jace B. King, Ryan Kellems, David N. Top Jr., et al. "Functional MRI Connectivity of Children With Autism and Low Verbal and Cognitive Performance." *Molecular Autism* 9, no. 67 (2018). https://doi.org/10.1186/s13229-018-0248-y.

Grandin, Temple, and Richard Panek. *The Autistic Brain: Helping Different Kinds of Minds Succeed*. (Boston: Mariner Books, 2013).

Griswold, Ann. "Large Swedish Study Ties Autism to Early Death."
    Spectrum News. December 11, 2015.
    https://www.spectrumnews.org/news/large-swedish-study-
    ties-autism-to-early-death/.

Herman, Ellen. "HANS ASPERGER, '"AUTISTIC PSYCHOPATHY" IN
    CHILDHOOD,' 1944." The Autism History Project. 2019.
    https://blogs.uoregon.edu/autismhistoryproject/archive/ha
    ns-asperger-autistic-psychopathy-in-childhood-1944/.

Herman, Ellen. "LEO KANNER, 1894-1981." The Autism History
    Project. 2019.
    https://blogs.uoregon.edu/autismhistoryproject/people/leo
    -kanner-1894-1981/.

Hughes, James E. A., Jamie Ward, Elin Gruffydd, Simon Baron-
    Cohen, Paula Smith, Carrie Allison, and Julia Simner.
    "Savant Syndrome has a Distinct Psychological Profile in
    Autism," *Molecular Autism* 9, no. 53 (October 2018).
    https://doi.org/10.1186/s13229-018-0237-1.

Kanner, Leo. "Autistic Disturbances of Affective Contact." *Nervous
    Child*, no. 2 (1943): 217-50.
    http://simonsfoundation.s3.amazonaws.com/share/071207-
    leo-kanner-autistic-affective-contact.pdf.

Merriam-Webster Online. "Autism." Accessed February 21, 2022.
    https://www.merriam-webster.com/dictionary/autism.

Rudy, Lisa Jo. "Understanding the Three Levels of Autism." Verywell
    Health. Last modified October 30, 2021.
    https://www.verywellhealth.com/what-are-the-three-
    levels-of-autism-260233#level-3-requiring-very-substantial-
    support.

Schmidt, Rebecca, Nadine Nippe, Klaus Strobel, Max Masthoff, Olga
    Reifschneider, Daniela Delli Castelli, Carsten Höltke, et al.
    "Highly Shifted Proton MR Imaging: Cell Tracking by Using
    Direct Detection of Paramagnetic Compounds." *Radiology*
    272, no. 3 (August 2014): 615-7.
    https://doi.org/10.1148/radiol.14132056.

Trafton, Anne. "Calcium-based MRI Sensor Enables More Sensitive
    Brain Imaging." MIT News. April 30, 2018.
    https://news.mit.edu/2018/calcium-based-mri-sensor-
    enables-more-sensitive-brain-imaging-0430.

USAFacts. "State of US Population and Death Statistics." Accessed
    February 21, 2022. https://usafacts.org/state-of-the-
    union/population/?utm_source=bing&utm_medium=cpc&utm
    _campaign=ND-
    StatsData&msclkid=e046eef2199e1a134ef98fbaeee9e374.

Wikipedia. "Dallas-Fort Worth Metroplex." Last modified February 9,
    2022.
    https://en.wikipedia.org/wiki/Dallas%E2%80%93Fort_Worth_
    metroplex.

Wikipedia. "History of Asperger Syndrome." Last modified February
    16, 2022.
    https://en.wikipedia.org/wiki/History_of_Asperger_syndrom
    e.

Wikipedia. "Leo Kanner." Last modified February 21, 2022.
    https://en.wikipedia.org/wiki/Leo_Kanner#.

Wikipedia. "Refrigerator Mother Theory." Last modified January 23, 2022. https://en.wikipedia.org/wiki/Refrigerator_mother_theory.

Printed in Great Britain
by Amazon